D0902346

Night
&
Sleep

Rumi

Versions by
Coleman Barks & Robert Bly

ISBN 0-938756-01-X (Signed limited edition)
ISBN 0-938756-02-8 (Paperback)

Typeset by Ed Hogan/Aspect Composition
13 Robinson St., Somerville, Mass. 02145

Yellow Moon Press
P.O. Box 1316
Cambridge, MA 02238

*Thank you for the gifts of love
that make up this book.*

YELLOW MOON PRESS

The Mystery

The mystery does not get clearer by repeating the question.
Nor is it bought with going to amazing places.
Until you've kept your eyes and your wanting still for fifty years.
You don't begin to cross over from confusion.

WHY RUMI DIDN'T SIGN HIS POEMS

The most important event in Rumi's life (Sept. 30, 1207 - Dec. 17, 1273) was his meeting with Shams of Tabriz, but that didn't occur until Rumi was thirty-seven.

Rumi was born in Balkh, in what is now Afghanistan, a city then under the threat of Mongol invasion. His family soon fled that danger and began a journey that lasted sixteen years and ended at Konya in Turkey. Rumi's father and grandfather, and for generations beyond, had been scholars, theologians, and jurists, bookishly, conventionally, devout men. His father, Baha'u'ddin Walad, became a teacher in Konya under the royal patronage. At his death in 1228 Rumi inherited his father's library and position. In 1230, Burhan al-din Mahaqqiq, a dervish who had lived for years in solitude in the mountains, began to initiate Rumi into the mysteries of the Sufi teachings. For the next nine years the two of them traveled about the Near East, to Aleppo, to Damascus. When Burhan died in 1239, Rumi returned to Konya to take up his father's position.

Rumi would not have been interested in such details. Like most mystics, he could step aside from personal history, his alma mater, and his vita. The personal self for Rumi has no more importance than a minute speck on the presence of another reality. Rumi dove into that ocean when he met Shams.

In 1244 Shams appeared out of the desert, a wandering ecstatic, probably an artisan of some sort. He wore a ragged black wool cloak, his only possession. He was called Parinda, the winged one. Immediately, he galvanized Rumi's extensive knowledge into a passionate way. The story is told of Shams' taking Rumi's books and throwing them into a fishpond. "Now you must live what you know." Rumi moved to save his books. Shams explained that theoretical knowledge was not real but that if Rumi wanted the books, they could retrieve them together and dry them off. Rumi understood.

Shams was the "hidden saint" that Rumi had been searching for. Rumi's son, Sultan Walad, describes the friendship as being like that of Moses and Khadir, the chief guide of pilgrims on the path toward God. Shams and Rumi disappeared for weeks together. It was a union in which distinctions vanished. "Even the phrase each other doesn't make any sense."

Rumi's disciples were disturbed over this friendship that so totally occupied their teacher. Shams was driven away, to Damascus, for two years. Then Rumi sent for Shams, and the disciples again plotted. In May of 1247 they ambushed Shams. As they stabbed at him, he cried out to them the constant remembering of God, "There is only God. You are God." The story goes, that the consciousness of the ambushers was so struck by this that they fell insensible to the ground. When they awoke, there were a few drops of blood, but the body of Shams had vanished. No trace of him was ever found.

After the disappearance of Shams, poetry began to flow from Rumi. Quatrains and odes sprang from him, as prayer and teaching and song, whenever he was with his students. They recorded the spontaneous words and afterwards chanted them during the Sufi dances.

The short poems, as well as the mystical odes, are often without what might be called logical cohesion. They have the unity that comes from a practicing, passionately honest, devotion. They are practical, rather than consistent. They are wry and ecstatic. Occasional and spontaneous, unrevised, oral.

Rumi himself was not primarily interested in poetry. It was a way of being with his friends. "It's necessary. As when a man must reach his hands into tripe and wash it and prepare it for his guest, because that's what his guest has asked for." These are love poems. The most important "doctrine" in them is that of the Friend. Beloved, the Soul, that close presence which all spiritual capitalization despairs of. Rumi's life was transformed, at thirty-seven, by the love-knowledge and unity that came to him with the appearance of Shams. After that, Rumi's life was no longer his own. He was absorbed into an incandescent love. He could no longer, for example, sign his name to claim his own writings. His collection of odes is entitled Divani Shamsi Tabriz, *The Works of Shams of Tabriz. The* Mathnawi *he calls "The Book of Husam," a favorite student. This was not an affectation. Rumi became the instrument, not the source. He was the reed made into a flute. The breath, and the music, was from elsewhere.*

For Rumi, poetry involves a sacred doubleness, a constant, loving, straying conversation—a longing to be the Friend. The poems fill with questions, images of conscious distance:

How is it with this love,
I see your world, and not you?

Who looks out with my eyes?

There often seems to be something missing from a Rumi poem, a space. This is the center of longing in each of them. "You must fill it with yourself."

Coleman Barks
Oct. 26, 1980

Night
&
Sleep

Night and Sleep

At the time of night-prayer, as the sun slides down,
the route the senses walk on closes, the route to the invisible opens.

The angel of sleep then gathers and drives along the spirits;
just as the mountain keeper gathers his sheep on a slope.

And what amazing sights he offers to the descending sheep!
Cities with sparkling streets, hyacinth gardens, emerald pastures!

The spirit sees astounding beings, turtles turned to men,
men turned to angels, when sleep erases the banal.

I think one could say the spirit goes back to its old home;
it no longer remembers where it lives, and loses its fatigue.

It carries around in life so many griefs and loads
and trembles under their weight; they are gone, it is all well.

Maybe They're Shy

Now the nightbirds will be singing
of the way we love each other.

Why should they sing about flowers
when they've seen us in the garden?

Maybe they're shy. They can't look at the face,
so they describe feet.

If they keep dividing love into pieces,
they'll disappear altogether. We must be gentle
and explain it to them.

Think of a mountain so huge the Caucasus Range
is a tiny speck. Normal mountains
run toward her when she calls.

They listen in their cave-ears and echo back.
They turn upsidedown when they get close,
they're so excited.

No more words. In the name of this place we drink in
with our breathing, stay quiet like a flower.
So the nightbirds will start singing.

Solomon and All His Wives

They try to say what you are, spiritual or sexual?
They wonder about Solomon and all his wives.
In the body of the world, they say, there is a soul, and you are that.
But we have ways within each other that will never be said by anyone.

Idle Questions

A person hit a Worker a good strong blow from behind.
The Worker swung around to return it; and the man said:
"Before you hit me, I have a question for you.
Now this is it: that sound: was it made by my hand or your neck?"
"The pain I am feeling does not give me leave for speculation.
These things are all right to worry about if you're feeling no pain."

The sufis are never ordained and do not believe that spiritual knowledge
can be spoken from a pulpit. The name they have for each other is
Worker.

Praising Manners

We should ask God
to help us toward manners. Inner gifts
do not find their way
to creatures without just respect.

If a man or woman flails about, he not only
smashes his house,
he burns the world down.

Your depression is connected to your insolence
and refusal to praise. Whoever feels himself walking
on the path, and refuses to praise—that man or woman
steals from others every day—is a shoplifter!

The sun became full of light when it got hold of itself.
Angels only began shining when they achieved discipline.
The sun goes out whenever the cloud of not-praising comes near.
The moment the foolish angel felt insolent, he heard the door close.

The Hidden

For a while we lived with people,
but we saw no sign in them of the faithfulness we wanted.
It's better to hide completely within
as water hides in metal, as fire hides in a rock.

Longing for the Birds of Solomon

Is this Stuff poetry? It's what birds sing in cages.
Where are the words spoken by the birds of Solomon?

How would you know their cries, if you heard them,
when you haven't seen Solomon even for two seconds?

That bird lifts his wings, one tip touches East, one West.
Those who hear the note feel an intensity in their whole body.

The bird descends from the Holy One's bedroom door to earth,
and from earth it flies among light back to the Great Seat.

Without Solomon every bird is a bat in love with darkness.
Listen oh mischievous bat, try to become his friend—do you want
                                    to stay in your cave forever?

If you go even three feet towards Solomon's mountain,
others will use that as a yardstick to measure their lives.

If your leg is gimpy, and you have to hop, what's the difference?
Going there, even by limping, the leg grows whole.

The Ears

The big ear on the outside of our head could be closed.
It is so good at hearing that the inner ear goes deaf.
What if you had no hearing at all, no nose, no mind-stuff!
Then one could hear well the three syllables: "Turn around."

Our sounds, our work, our renown, these are outer.
When we move inwardly, we move through inner space.
Our feet walk firmly, they experience sidewalks well.
There is one inside who walks like Jesus on the sea.

When Things Are Heard

The ear participates, and helps arrange marriages;
the eye has already made love with what it sees.

The eye knows pleasure, delights in the body's shape:
the ear hears words that talk about all this.

When hearing takes place, character areas change;
but when you see, inner areas change.

If all you know about fire is what you have heard
see if the fire will agree to cook you!

Certain energies come only when you burn.
If you long for belief, sit down in the fire!

When the ear receives subtly; it turns into an eye.
But if words do not reach the ear in the chest, nothing happens.

Who Says Words with My Mouth

All day I think about it, then at night I say it.

Where did I come from and what am I supposed to be doing?
I have no idea.

My soul is from elsewhere, I'm sure of that,
and I intend to end up there.

This drunkenness began in some other tavern.
When I get back around to that place,
I'll be completely sober. Meanwhile,

I'm like a bird from another continent, sitting in this aviary.
The day is coming when I fly off,

but who is it now in my ear, who hears my voice?
Who says words with my mouth?

Who looks out with my eyes? What is the soul?
I cannot stop asking.

If I could taste one sip of an answer,
I could break out of this prison for drunks.

I didn't come here of my own accord, and I can't leave that way.
Let whoever brought me here take me back.

This poetry. I never know what I'm going to say.
I don't plan it.

When I'm outside the saying of it,
I get very quiet and rarely speak at all.

The Friend

Friend, our closeness is this:
Anywhere you put your foot, feel me in the firmness under you.

How is it with this love.
I see your world and not you?

Someone Digging in the Ground

An eye is meant to see things.
The soul is here for its own joy.

A head has one use: For loving a true love.
Feet: To chase after.

Love is for vanishing into the sky. The mind,
for learning what men have done and tried to do.

Mysteries are not to be solved: The eye goes blind
when it only wants to see why.

A lover is always accused of something.
But when he finds his love, whatever was lost
in the looking comes back completely changed.

On the way to Mecca, many dangers: Thieves,
the blowing wind, and only camel's milk to drink.

Still, each pilgrim kisses the black stone there
with pure longing, feeling in the surface
the taste of the lips he wants.

This talk is like stamping new coins. They pile up,
while the real work is done outside
by someone digging in the ground.

The Ground

Today, like every other day, we wake up empty and scared.
Don't open the door to the study and begin reading.
Take down the dulcimer.

Let the beauty we love be what we do.
There are hundreds of ways to kneel and kiss the ground.

No Wall

The clear bead at the center changes everything.
There are no edges to my loving now.
I've heard it said, there's a window that opens from one mind to another,
but if there's no wall, there's no need for fitting the window, or the latch.

The Instruments

Who is the luckiest in this whole orchestra? The reed.
Its mouth touches your lips to learn music.

All reeds, sugarcane especially, think only
of this chance. They sway in the canebrakes,
free in the many ways they dance.

Without you the instruments would die.
One sits close beside you. Another takes a long kiss.
The tambourine begs, Touch my skin so I can be myself.

Let me feel you enter each limb bone by bone,
that what died last night can be whole today.

Why live some soberer way, and feel you ebbing out?
I won't do it.

Either give me enough wine or leave me alone,
now that I know how it is
to be with you in a constant conversation.

The Elusive Ones

They're lovers again: Sugar dissolving in milk.

Day and night, no difference. The sun is the moon:
An amalgam. Their gold and silver melt together.

This is the season when the dead branch and the green
branch are the same branch.

The cynic bites his finger because he can't understand.
Omar and Ali on the same throne, two kings
in one belt!

Nightmares fill with light like a holiday.
Men and angels speak one language.
The elusive ones finally meet.

The essence and evolving forms
run to meet each other like children
to their father and mother.

Good and evil, dead and alive, everything blooms
from one natural stem.

You know this already, I'll stop.
Any direction you turn it's one vision.

Shams, my body is a candle touched with fire.

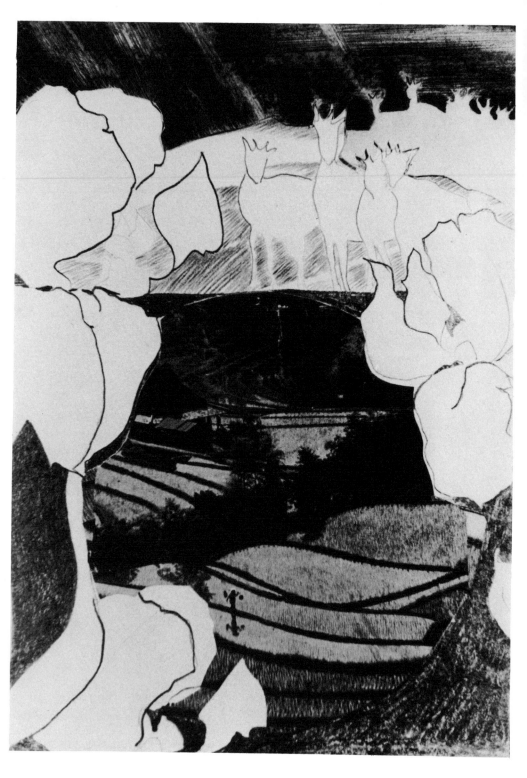

Across the Doorsill

The breeze at dawn has secrets to tell you. Don't go back to sleep!
You must ask for what you really want. Don't go back to sleep!
People are going back and forth across the doorsill where
the two worlds touch.
The door is round and open. Don't go back to sleep!

Notes on the Versions

Coleman Barks' versions are the result of collaborating with John Moyne. Literal Persian translations by Moyne provide the base for the versions by Barks. The versions by Coleman Barks are: "The Mystery," "Maybe They're Shy," "Solomon and All His Wives," "The Hidden," "Who Says Words with My Mouth," "The Friend," "Someone Digging in the Ground," "The Ground," "No Wall," "The Instruments," "The Elusive Ones," & "Across the Doorsill."

Robert Bly's versions come from his work with the translations of the late British professor of Persian, A. J. Arberry, & Reynold A. Nicholson. The versions by Robert Bly are: "Night & Sleep," "Idle Questions," "Praising Manners," "Longing for the Birds of Solomon," "The Ears," & "When Things Are Heard."

Notes on the Gift Givers

Coleman Barks was born in Chattanooga, Tennessee on April 23, 1937. He now teaches poetry at the University of Georgia. He has published one book of poems, The Juice *(Harper & Row) and two chapbooks from small presses,* New Words *(Burnt Hickory) &* We're Laughing at the Damage *(Briarpatch). He received an NEA grant for 1979-80. "Someone Digging in the Ground" from this collection will also appear in the Spring issue of* Water Table *in Seattle, Washington.*

Robert Bly has been a major force in American poetry for two decades both as poet & translator. He received the National Book Award for his collection of poems, Light Around the Body. *His translations include Nobel Laureates Pablo Neruda & Vicente Aleixandre; the ecstatic poets Kabir & Mirabai, as well as Rainer Maria Rilke & others. His most recent publication is:* News of the Universe, *poems of twofold consciousness (Sierra Club Books). He lives in Moose Lake, Minnesota.*

Laurie Graybeal, a graphic designer living in Charlotte, N.C. did the calligraphy for the cover & title page.

John Moyne is a Persian scholar who has published widely in the field of Persian grammar & linguistics. Rumi's poetry has long been a great love of his. Currently, he is chairman of the Department of Computer Science at CUNY.

Rita Shumaker specializes in interdisciplinary work between the arts & psychology. She believes that Metaphor & Symbol remain mysterious as they create a bridge between the physical & spiritual realms of human experience. Her work has been exhibited throughout the Southeast, Washington, D.C., New York State & Texas. She has been an Artist In Residence for the past six years at the annual Conference on The Great Mother & The New Father. Also, she has run workshops at Beloit College, Denison University, Assumption College, & with the South Carolina Visiting Artist Program. She lives in Charlotte, N.C. & teaches at Piedmont Community College & Belmont Abbey College.